Pits to Parks

Written by Jan Burchett and Sara Vogler

Collins

This was a rubbish tip.

Now look!

This pit was full of rocks.

Now you can zip in the air.

This part of town was run-down.

Now it is a sheep farm.

Coal was dug up at this pit.

Now it is a park.

This was a coalpit too.

Now look!

This deep pit ...

... is now a garden with a high roof.

Soil was dug up at this pit.

Now you can sail!

Jobs

17

Rubbish to ... parks

Tip to park

Turn it!

🐾 Review: After reading 🐾

Use your assessment from hearing the children read to choose any GPCs, words or tricky words that need additional practice.

Read 1: Decoding

- On page 6, point to the phrase **run-down**. Ask: In what ways is this land **run-down**? (e.g. *left to get overgrown*; *not fixed up*)
- Help the children to sound out as they read the following. Ask: Can you see the digraphs? What sounds do they make?

  run-down (*ow*)   **look** (*oo*)   **roof** (*oo*)

  rubbish (*bb, sh*)   **coalpit** (*oa*)   **garden** (*ar*)

- On page 7, point to words that contain a long vowel phoneme (e.g. **farm**, **sheep**). Say: Can you blend in your head, silently, before you read these words out loud?

Read 2: Prosody

- Turn to pages 10 and 11. Discuss which words to emphasise to link the meaning with the pages before. (e.g. *emphasise* **too** *and* **Now**)
- Ask the children to read pages 10 and 11, experimenting with emphasis to make the links, making the change from the past to present clear.
- Challenge the children to read the new captions fluently.
- Bonus content: Work as a group to think of a caption for each photo on pages 16 and 17, focusing on each job (e.g. *planning the park*; *digging soil*; *sowing seeds, etc*).

Read 3: Comprehension

- Can the children describe any ugly places or old rubbish tips they have seen. Ask: What would you like them to be now?
- Discuss who or what benefits from changing tips into parks, and why (e.g. *people get space for outdoor fun*; *trees and other wildlife can grow*).
- On pages 22 and 23, ask the children to talk about what had to happen to each of the places in the left-hand pictures, to turn them into the places on the right.
- Bonus content: Turn to pages 20 and 21, and ask the children to predict what happens at each stage of the change from pit to park, and what happens after park opens.